AF413514

THE BOUNDLESS CLASSROOM

INNOVATIONS IN GLOBAL EDUCATION

DR. MINAKSHI BANSAL

Contents

Contents

Prayer

"Om Bhadram Karnebhih Shrinuyama Devah
Bhadram Pashyemakshabhiryajatrah
Sthirairangais Tushtuvamsastanubhih
Vyashema Devahitam Yadayuh
Svasti Na Indro Vriddhashravah
Svasti Nah Pusha Vishwavedah
Svasti Nastarkshyo Arishtanemih
Svasti No Brihaspatir Dadhatu
Om Shantih Shantih Shantih"

This mantra is a prayer for universal well-being, invoking the blessings of various deities for protection, health, and happiness. It emphasizes the importance of experiencing the auspicious through all senses and living a life aligned with divine purpose. The repetition of "Shantih" at the end signifies a deep desire for peace in the individual, the environment, and the universe at large. This mantra is often recited as a prayer for peace, prosperity, and the physical and spiritual well-being of all beings.

ᘇᘇᘇ

About The Author

Dr. Minakshi Bansal, born in the bustling metropolis of Delhi, India, has led a life steeped in artistry, scholarly pursuit, and an unwavering commitment to societal betterment. Following her marriage, she relocated to Ahmedabad, Gujarat, where she has since blossomed into a multifaceted beacon of inspiration for many. Dr. Minakshi is not only recognized as a gifted artist in the realm of Fine Arts but also as an esteemed author, a devoted social worker and a dedicated research scholar in Psychology. Her journey, marked by a profound dedication to elevating those around her, especially the downtrodden and underprivileged children of society, is a testament to her deep-seated belief in the transformative power of engagement and empathy.

From her earliest days, Minakshi was distinguished by an insatiable appetite for reading. Her literary universe was inhabited by characters and narratives that spanned ethical tales, motivational and inspirational stories, and the mythic parables imbued with life lessons. This voracious reading habit was not merely for personal edification but was driven by a desire to distill and disseminate the essence of these narratives to foster the development of students and peers alike. She was particularly captivated by the lives and teachings of historical figures and spiritual leaders such as Adi Shankaracharya, Swami Vivekananda, Dr. APJ Abdul Kalam, Mahamana Pandit Madan Mohan Malviya, Mahatma Gandhi, Sardar Vallabhai Patel, and Vinoba Bhave, among others. Their philosophies and life stories fueled her ambition to embody their ideals of resilience, selflessness, and relentless pursuit of knowledge.

Dr. Minakshi's academic and practical engagement with psychology has been equally noteworthy. As a research scholar, her focus has been on exploring the intricate tapestry of the human psyche, aiming to unlock the potential for psychological well-being and societal harmony. Her scholarly work is complemented by her active involvement in social work, where she employs her academic insights to make tangible differences in the lives of the underprivileged. Her endeavours in social work are characterized by an innovative approach that combines traditional wisdom with contemporary psychological practices to address the multifaceted challenges faced by these communities.

Her artistic talents, another facet of her diverse capabilities, are not merely a personal passion but also serve as a medium through which she communicates and connects with others. Her art, rich in symbolism and emotional depth, reflects her philosophical inquiries and social concerns, offering viewers a glimpse into the breadth of her intellect and the depth of her compassion.

In addition to her contributions to the arts and social sciences, Dr. Minakshi has embraced the healing arts of Pranic Healing, mastering the techniques developed by Master Choa Kok Sui. This practice, which focuses on the manipulation of Prana or life energy to heal the body and aura, has been both a personal journey of discovery and a means through which she extends her healing touch to others. Her proficiency in Pranic Healing is complemented by her advocacy and teaching of various forms of meditation aimed at rejuvenation, personal betterment, and the cultivation of harmony within individuals and communities alike.

Dr. Minakshi's life is a narrative of relentless pursuit, not just of personal achievement but of the upliftment and empowerment of society at large. Her diverse interests and talents—spanning the arts, literature, psychology, and the healing practices—converge on a singular path of service. She embodies the spirit of the luminaries who inspired her, channelling their legacy through her actions and teachings. Through her books, art, and social initiatives, she continues to inspire a new generation to embark on their own journeys of self-discovery, resilience, and altruism.

Her commitment to social betterment, particularly her focus on uplifting underprivileged children, reflects a deep understanding of the transformative potential of education and personal development. By integrating her knowledge of psychology, her artistic sensibilities, and her healing practices, Dr. Bansal has developed a holistic approach to social work that addresses both the immediate needs and the long-term well-being of the communities she serves.

As an author, Dr. Minakshi's writings offer a blend of inspirational insights, practical wisdom, and reflective contemplations drawn from her extensive reading and life experiences. Her books serve as a guide for those seeking to navigate the complexities of life with grace, resilience, and purpose. Through her narratives, she extends an invitation to her readers to explore the depths of their own potential and to contribute meaningfully to the collective well-being of society.

In Dr. Minakshi Bansal, we find a remarkable synthesis of the artist, the scholar, the healer, and the social activist. Her life's work stands as a beacon of hope and a source of inspiration for individuals seeking to make a difference in the world. Her story is a compelling reminder of the power of individual action, rooted in compassion and driven by a profound commitment to the betterment of humanity. Dr. Minakshi's legacy is not just in the tangible outcomes of her efforts but in the enduring spirit of inquiry, empathy, and service that she embodies.

ৡৡৡ

Preface

Education is a cornerstone of human society, shaping the lives of individuals and the trajectory of nations. It is through education that we acquire the knowledge, skills, and values necessary to navigate the complexities of the modern world and to contribute meaningfully to society. As an educator myself, I have long been passionate about the transformative power of education and the potential it holds to unlock opportunities and change lives.

In this book, I aim to explore the evolving landscape of education in the 21st century and to showcase the innovative approaches and practices that are shaping the future of learning worldwide. Drawing on my own experiences as an educator, as well as insights and perspectives from experts and practitioners across the field, I seek to provide a comprehensive overview of the key trends, challenges, and opportunities facing education today.

In an increasingly interconnected and globalized world, the traditional notion of the classroom as a physical space with four walls is giving way to a more expansive vision of education—one that extends beyond the confines of the school building and embraces the diverse contexts and communities in which learning takes place.

Throughout the pages of this book, I will explore a wide range of topics and innovations that are shaping the future of education, from the digital revolution to personalized learning, from gamification to virtual reality. Each chapter will delve into a different aspect of education, highlighting key trends, best practices, and real-world examples from around the globe. My hope is that by shining a spotlight on these innovations, we can inspire educators, policymakers, and stakeholders to embrace new approaches and to work together to create a more equitable, inclusive, and effective educational system for all.

As the author of this book, I bring to the table my own perspectives and experiences as an educator, but I also recognize the importance of collaboration and dialogue in shaping the future of education. That is why I have sought to incorporate diverse voices and perspectives throughout the book, drawing on insights and expertise from educators, researchers, policymakers, and practitioners from a variety of backgrounds and contexts. By bringing together these diverse perspectives, I hope to provide a more comprehensive and nuanced understanding of the complex issues and challenges facing education today.

It is my sincere hope that this book will serve as a valuable resource for educators, policymakers, researchers, and anyone else with an interest in the future of education. Whether you are a seasoned educator looking for new ideas and inspiration, a policymaker seeking innovative solutions to pressing challenges, or a concerned citizen eager to contribute to positive change, I hope that you will find something of value within these pages.

Dr. Minakshi Bansal
Social Activist
Ahmedabad, Gujarat, Bharat

ᏞᏞᏞ

ONE

THE DIGITAL REVOLUTION: TRANSFORMING LEARNING SPACES

The digital revolution has fundamentally transformed the concept of learning spaces, reshaping how education is delivered and accessed across the globe. Traditionally, learning was confined to physical classrooms, where students and teachers interacted face-to-face. However, with the advent of digital technologies, the boundaries of these spaces have expanded, enabling a dynamic and interactive learning environment that transcends geographical and physical limitations.

One of the most significant changes brought about by the digital revolution is the shift towards online learning platforms. These platforms offer a plethora of resources and tools that facilitate both synchronous and asynchronous learning. Students can now access lectures, course materials, and assignments at their convenience, allowing for a more personalized and flexible learning experience. Furthermore, these platforms often incorporate interactive elements such as forums, quizzes, and videos, making learning more engaging and effective.

The integration of digital tools in education has also led to the emergence of virtual classrooms. These are not merely platforms for delivering content but are interactive spaces where students can collaborate, discuss, and share ideas, just as they would in a physical classroom. Technologies such as video conferencing and real-time document editing enable live discussions and group projects, fostering a sense of community and collaboration among students from diverse backgrounds.

Moreover, the digital revolution has facilitated the adoption of innovative teaching methodologies. For example, flipped classrooms, where students review content at home and engage in problem-solving activities in class, are gaining popularity. This method leverages digital content for learning outside the classroom, while class time is devoted to deeper engagement with the material through discussions and practical applications. This shift not only enhances learning outcomes but also encourages active participation and critical thinking among students.

Another pivotal aspect of the digital transformation in education is the accessibility it provides. Digital learning tools have made education more inclusive by offering learning opportunities to individuals who may have been excluded due to geographical, financial, or physical constraints. Online courses and digital resources are often less costly than traditional education methods and can be accessed by anyone with an internet connection. This democratization of education has the potential to bridge educational disparities and foster a more equitable learning environment.

Furthermore, the use of data analytics in education is a byproduct of the digital revolution that is having a profound impact.

Educational institutions and educators can now track student engagement, performance, and learning patterns in real time. This data is invaluable as it allows for a more tailored educational experience that can adapt to the needs of individual students. Analyzing this data helps in identifying areas where students struggle, allowing for timely interventions that can significantly enhance the learning process.

However, the transition to digital learning spaces is not without challenges. Issues such as digital literacy, access to reliable internet, and the availability of suitable devices are significant barriers that need to be addressed to fully harness the potential of digital education. Additionally, there is a growing concern about the digital divide, as those without access to technology are at risk of being left behind in an increasingly digital world.

The digital revolution has transformed traditional learning spaces, introducing a new era of education characterized by flexibility, inclusivity, and interactivity. While there are challenges to be overcome, the opportunities provided by digital education platforms are vast and hold the promise of shaping a more informed, engaged, and equitable global citizenry. As the digital landscape continues to evolve, it will undoubtedly continue to influence how education is conceptualized and delivered in the future.

ݒݒݒ

"Education is the key that unlocks the boundless potential within every learner, transcending borders and transforming lives."

♥♥♥

TWO
GLOBAL CONNECTIVITY: LINKING CLASSROOMS ACROSS CONTINENTS

Global connectivity is revolutionizing education by linking classrooms across continents, thereby fostering a truly international learning experience. This transformative approach not only broadens the educational horizons of students but also equips them with the skills necessary to thrive in a globally interconnected world. Through various technological platforms and collaborative programs, students from vastly different cultural, economic, and geographical backgrounds are able to connect, interact, and learn from each other.

The foundation of global connectivity in education lies in the use of the internet and communication technologies. Tools such as video conferencing, online collaborative spaces, and real-time messaging have broken down the traditional barriers that once limited educational exchanges to physical travel.

Now, a classroom in a small village in Africa can seamlessly connect with a classroom in a bustling city in Europe. This level of interaction exposes students to diverse perspectives and enhances their understanding of different cultures and societies.

One of the key benefits of linking classrooms across continents is the enhancement of cultural literacy among students. In these globally connected classrooms, students engage in joint projects and discussions that require them to negotiate, collaborate, and communicate across cultural boundaries. For instance, students can participate in global science fairs, international debates, and cross-cultural literature circles, activities that not only enhance academic skills but also build empathy, respect, and an appreciation for diversity.

Furthermore, global connectivity allows for the sharing of educational resources and expertise that might not be available locally. Schools in less developed regions can benefit from access to high-quality teaching resources, expert lectures, and specialized knowledge from more affluent countries. Conversely, students in developed countries gain insights into emerging markets, sustainable practices, and alternative approaches to problem-solving that are practiced in different parts of the world. This reciprocal relationship enriches the educational experience for all parties involved.

Language learning has also been profoundly impacted by global connectivity. The ability to connect with native speakers and immerse oneself in the language environment without leaving the classroom is an invaluable resource. Language students can engage in real-time conversations with peers from the target language country, participate in cultural exchanges, and practice language skills in authentic contexts. This approach not only accelerates language acquisition but also deepens cultural understanding.

Another significant aspect of global connectivity is the professional development it offers teachers. Educators can participate in international training programs, online professional courses, and global teaching communities.

These opportunities enable teachers to learn new pedagogical strategies, stay updated on educational trends, and develop a global teaching perspective. This professional growth translates into more effective teaching practices and a better learning experience for students.

Despite its numerous benefits, the implementation of global connectivity in education faces several challenges. The disparity in technological infrastructure between developed and developing countries can hinder effective communication and collaboration.

Additionally, time zone differences and language barriers can complicate synchronous interactions and require innovative solutions and flexible scheduling. Ensuring cyber safety and managing data privacy are also critical concerns that need to be addressed as students and teachers engage in online interactions.

The impact of global connectivity on education is profound and far-reaching. It not only transforms the way educational content is delivered but also reshapes the educational objectives towards creating a more interconnected and empathetic global citizenry. As technology advances and more educational institutions embrace global connectivity, the potential for innovative educational practices and worldwide collaboration is boundless.

With careful planning and thoughtful implementation, the linking of classrooms across continents will continue to break down cultural and geographical barriers, offering students a rich and diverse educational experience that prepares them for the challenges and opportunities of a globalized world.

❧❧❧

*"In the boundless classroom of the future,
innovation is not just a choice—it's a necessity for
navigating the complexities of the modern world."*

❥❥❥

THREE

Personalized Learning: Tailoring Education to Individual Needs

Personalized learning represents a significant shift from the traditional one-size-fits-all approach to education, emphasizing the tailoring of pedagogy, curriculum, and learning environments to meet the diverse needs of individual students. This approach leverages technological advancements to create educational experiences that are not only more engaging but also more effective at addressing the unique strengths, weaknesses, interests, and goals of each student.

At the heart of personalized learning is the use of technology to gather and analyze data on individual learning patterns. Educational software and platforms can track progress, identify areas of strength and difficulty, and adapt in real-time to challenge students appropriately while providing the support they need. For example, adaptive learning technologies can modify the content, pace, and difficulty of material as students work through modules, providing a truly customized learning experience that is designed to optimize their learning outcomes.

Furthermore, personalized learning extends beyond just academic content. It also involves tailoring learning strategies to the preferred styles of learners. Some students may benefit from visual learning aids, such as infographics and video, while others might find interactive simulations or text-based content more effective. By allowing students to access learning in the format that best suits their natural preferences, engagement and comprehension can significantly improve.

Personalized learning also considers the pace at which a student learns best. In traditional classrooms, all students move through material at the same pace, regardless of their individual needs. This can lead to advanced learners feeling bored and unchallenged and struggling learners feeling overwhelmed and discouraged. Personalized learning environments allow students to progress through lessons at their own pace, spending more time on challenging areas and less on those they master quickly. This approach not only enhances learning by reducing frustration and boredom but also encourages students to take ownership of their educational journeys.

Moreover, personalized learning can help in setting personalized goals. Educators can work closely with students to set achievable, yet challenging, goals that are tailored to their personal academic and career aspirations.

This aspect of personalized learning not only motivates students but also makes their education more relevant to their future plans. Regular check-ins and updates on these goals keep the learning process dynamic and responsive to the student's development and changing interests.

The role of the teacher in a personalized learning environment also shifts from that of a mere transmitter of knowledge to that of a guide or coach. Teachers use the insights gained from data analytics to intervene strategically in their students' learning processes, providing targeted feedback and support where necessary.

This can include one-on-one tutoring sessions, group work designed to address specific needs, or directed independent study. The teacher becomes a facilitator of a more personalized learning experience, rather than the central figure in a traditional lecture-based classroom.

Implementing personalized learning does come with challenges, particularly in terms of scalability and resource allocation. Schools must have access to the necessary technological infrastructure and must be able to provide adequate training for educators to manage these new systems effectively.

Additionally, there is the risk of data privacy concerns, as significant amounts of student data are collected and analyzed. Ensuring the security of this data and using it ethically is paramount to maintaining trust and integrity in educational settings.

Personalized learning is transforming educational paradigms by making learning more responsive to the needs of the individual. It harnesses the power of technology to provide a richer, more engaging, and more effective educational experience. As educational technologies continue to evolve, the potential for even more advanced and nuanced personalization becomes apparent, promising a future where all students can achieve their full potential in ways that best suit their individual learning needs.

This approach not only fosters academic success but also supports the overall well-being and personal growth of students, preparing them to be competent and confident individuals in a diverse and ever-changing world.

ᐁᐁᐁ

"As educators, we have the power to shape the
future by nurturing the critical thinking, creativity,
and resilience of every student."

❦❦❦

FOUR

GAMIFICATION IN EDUCATION: LEARNING THROUGH PLAY

Gamification in education is a transformative approach that incorporates game design elements into learning environments to enhance engagement, motivation, and acquisition of knowledge. By integrating the mechanics of games into educational activities, gamification seeks to harness the intrinsic motivation that games can generate, making learning more enjoyable and effective. This innovative method has gained significant traction in recent years as educators and institutions look for new ways to meet the diverse needs of students in an increasingly digital world.

At its core, gamification involves the application of game-based elements, such as point scoring, competition with others, and rules of play, to educational activities. These elements are not merely added to the existing curriculum superficially; rather, they are integrated into the educational content to create a cohesive and engaging learning experience.

For instance, a history lesson could be transformed into a quest where students earn points or badges for completing tasks like identifying historical figures or explaining significant events. This not only makes the lesson more engaging but also allows students to see their progress in real time, which can be incredibly motivating.

One of the key benefits of gamification is its ability to increase student engagement. Traditional educational methods can sometimes fail to capture students' attention and interest, especially with the increasing competition from numerous digital distractions. Gamification leverages the compelling nature of games to capture and hold students' interest. Elements such as challenges, levels, and immediate feedback keep students involved and focused, making it more likely that they will absorb the material being taught.

Furthermore, gamification promotes a growth mindset by encouraging students to view challenges as opportunities to learn and grow, rather than obstacles. In many games, failing is seen as a part of the learning process—a way to learn from mistakes and improve.

When this approach is applied to education, students are more likely to persist through difficulties and develop resilience. This is particularly beneficial in educational settings where fear of failure can significantly hinder learning.

Gamification also facilitates personalized learning, allowing students to progress at their own pace. In a gamified environment, learners can choose paths that suit their learning style and interests. For instance, a student who is particularly interested in certain aspects of a subject can choose to explore deeper into that area, earning special badges or rewards for doing so. This level of autonomy and choice can lead to a more satisfying and customized educational experience.

Collaboration is another significant aspect of gamification. Many educational games are designed to be played in groups or teams, which encourages students to work together to solve problems or complete tasks. This collaborative environment not only helps students learn from each other but also fosters social skills such as communication, negotiation, and cooperation. Such skills are crucial for personal and professional success beyond the classroom.

Moreover, gamification provides immediate feedback, a critical component of effective learning. Traditional educational assessments often involve delayed feedback, such as tests or papers graded days or weeks after they are completed. In contrast, gamified learning provides instant feedback on students' actions, allowing them to understand what they know and what they need to focus on immediately. This immediacy helps keep students engaged and on track with their learning objectives.

Despite its benefits, gamification in education is not without challenges. Designing effective gamified learning experiences requires a deep understanding of both game design and educational objectives. Poorly implemented gamification can feel superficial or gimmicky, potentially detracting from the learning experience rather than enhancing it.

Furthermore, there is the risk that the competitive elements of gamification could lead to negative feelings among students, such as frustration or anxiety, if not carefully managed.

Overall, gamification in education represents a dynamic and innovative approach to learning that can make educational experiences more engaging, interactive, and effective. As educators continue to explore and refine this approach, it has the potential to significantly transform educational practices, making learning more appealing and accessible to students of all ages and backgrounds.

This method not only supports academic achievement but also helps in developing a range of cognitive and social skills that are essential in the modern world.

ᐅᐅᐅ

"The digital revolution has transformed education,
turning the world into a boundless classroom where
knowledge knows no bounds."

❦❦❦

FIVE

Virtual Reality: Immersive Learning Environments

Virtual reality (VR) is dramatically transforming the educational landscape by creating immersive learning environments that enhance both engagement and understanding. This technology allows students to interact with three-dimensional environments in real time, providing experiences that are otherwise impossible within the confines of a traditional classroom. By donning VR headsets, learners can explore ancient civilizations, dissect complex biological structures, or even simulate chemical reactions, all within a controlled and interactive setting.

The essence of VR's impact on education lies in its ability to create a deep sense of presence and immersion. This immersion is a powerful tool for learning as it engages multiple senses, leading to increased attention and improved retention of information. For instance, instead of reading about the Battle of Gettysburg, students can experience the event as if they were there. They can look around, hear sounds from the battlefield, and understand the event in a context that textbooks alone cannot provide. This not only makes learning more interesting but also deepens the students' understanding by providing them a "first-hand" experience of the subject matter.

Moreover, VR can make complex or abstract concepts tangible. Subjects that traditionally require a strong imaginative ability, such as astronomy or quantum physics, can be visualized through VR. Students can walk on the surface of Mars or observe subatomic particles in motion, making these complex ideas easier to comprehend and much more fascinating. This ability to directly interact with educational content can demystify challenging subjects, making them more accessible to all students.

The benefits of VR also extend to skill development, particularly in fields where real-world training is either too dangerous, expensive, or impractical. For example, medical students using VR can perform surgical procedures in a risk-free environment. They can practice as many times as needed without the fear of making irreversible mistakes on actual patients. Similarly, VR can simulate electrical circuit assembly for engineering students or create immersive language learning experiences where students interact within a simulated foreign environment, practicing their language skills with virtual characters.

Personalized learning is another significant advantage of VR. It allows students to learn at their own pace and follow personalized pathways. For instance, in a VR-based learning module, students can choose to explore areas that interest them the most, spend additional time where they struggle, or skip over content they already understand. This adaptability helps meet the individual needs of each student, which is often difficult to achieve in a traditional classroom setting.

Collaboration in VR environments also offers unique opportunities. Students can work together in virtual spaces regardless of their physical location. This capability is particularly useful in fostering global collaboration, where students from different parts of the world can come together to solve problems, work on projects, or share knowledge. This not only enhances learning outcomes but also prepares students for a workforce that is increasingly global and digitally connected.

However, integrating VR into educational settings is not without challenges. The cost of VR equipment and the need for robust technical support can be significant barriers, particularly for under-resourced schools. There is also the risk of cognitive overload, where the richness of the VR environment might distract from learning objectives rather than enhancing them. Moreover, prolonged exposure to VR has been raised as a concern for causing physical discomfort, such as eye strain or motion sickness, which needs to be carefully managed.

Despite these challenges, the potential of VR in education is immense. It offers a highly engaging and effective way to deliver education, making learning an active rather than passive experience. As technology advances and becomes more affordable, it is likely that VR will become an increasingly common feature in educational institutions around the world.

Overall, virtual reality in education offers a fascinating glimpse into the future of learning. It provides a dynamic platform for immersive, interactive, and personalized learning experiences that can significantly enhance educational outcomes. By effectively leveraging this technology, educators can create compelling and transformative educational experiences that not only impart knowledge but also inspire a lifelong love of learning.

ppp

"Every child deserves access to a high-quality education, regardless of their background or circumstances."

❦❦❦

SIX
Artificial Intelligence: The New Teacher's Assistant

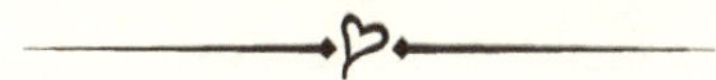

Artificial Intelligence (AI) is increasingly becoming an integral part of the educational landscape, acting as a new kind of teacher's assistant that transforms how teaching and learning occur. AI in education offers sophisticated tools that can assist with everything from administrative tasks to providing personalized learning experiences, making it a pivotal element in modern educational settings.

One of the primary roles of AI as a teacher's assistant is in the personalization of education. AI systems can analyze vast amounts of data on students' learning habits, preferences, and performance to tailor educational content to meet the needs of each individual student. For instance, AI can identify patterns in a student's learning behavior that might indicate when they are likely to struggle with a concept. The system can then automatically adjust the difficulty level of quizzes or introduce supplementary materials to help reinforce learning where it's needed most. This level of customization ensures that students receive support tailored specifically to their learning pace and style, which can enhance understanding and retention of information.

AI also significantly enhances the efficiency of assessment and grading. Teachers traditionally spend a considerable amount of time grading assignments and tests, a process that is not only time-consuming but also prone to inconsistencies. AI-driven systems can automate these tasks with high accuracy, freeing up teachers to spend more time on instructional duties and less on administrative tasks. These systems can handle everything from multiple-choice tests to more complex responses such as essays, providing detailed feedback that students can use to improve their understanding and performance.

Furthermore, AI can facilitate immersive learning experiences that are more interactive and engaging. For example, AI-powered virtual tutors can lead simulated conversations or learning activities, adapting their responses based on the interaction with the student. These tutors can provide immediate feedback, answer questions in real-time, and guide students through complex learning materials, effectively providing a one-on-one tutoring experience that is accessible anytime and anywhere.

AI also plays a crucial role in identifying and supporting students with special needs. By analyzing data on students' interactions and progress, AI can help identify learning disabilities or difficulties that might not be immediately apparent to human observers. Once these issues are identified, AI can recommend interventions tailored to the student's specific needs, such as suggesting alternative teaching methods or specialized resources. This proactive approach ensures that all students have the support they need to succeed academically.

Another significant benefit of AI in education is its ability to predict future learning outcomes and suggest interventions to improve those outcomes. By analyzing historical data and current performance, AI models can forecast how students are likely to perform in their courses and suggest actions to support their success. This predictive capability can be incredibly beneficial in higher education settings, where early identification of potential dropouts can lead to timely interventions that keep students on track for graduation.

However, integrating AI into educational environments is not without challenges. Ethical concerns, such as data privacy and the potential for bias in AI algorithms, are significant issues that need to be addressed. There is also the risk of over-reliance on technology, where the human aspect of education might be undervalued or overlooked. Ensuring that AI supports rather than replaces human interaction in education is crucial.

Despite these challenges, the potential of AI as a teacher's assistant is clear. It provides a powerful tool for enhancing educational practices, making learning more personalized, efficient, and engaging. As AI technology continues to evolve, its role in education is set to become even more significant, offering exciting possibilities for transforming teaching and learning processes. By leveraging AI effectively, educators can enrich the educational experience and better prepare students for the challenges of the future, ensuring that education is both inclusive and impactful.

ppp

"*Parental involvement is the cornerstone of a child's success, creating a strong support system that extends from home to school and beyond.*"

ᗐᗐᗐ

SEVEN

Sustainable Practices: Greening the Global Classroom

Sustainable practices in education, often referred to as "greening" the global classroom, involve the incorporation of environmentally friendly methods and resources into learning environments worldwide. This shift towards sustainability is critical in educating students not just academically but also in fostering a sense of environmental responsibility and stewardship. By integrating sustainable practices into classrooms, educational institutions can play a pivotal role in shaping a future where ecological awareness and action are at the forefront of global citizenship.

One of the fundamental ways schools are greening their classrooms is through the physical infrastructure of the buildings themselves. Many are adopting green building standards, utilizing materials and methods that reduce environmental impact. For instance, schools are being designed with energy efficiency in mind, incorporating solar panels, efficient lighting, and advanced heating, ventilation, and air conditioning systems that minimize energy use. Rainwater harvesting and greywater recycling are also becoming common, reducing water consumption and promoting water sustainability.

Beyond the physical, sustainable practices extend to the curriculum. Schools around the world are integrating environmental education into their syllabi, not as a standalone subject, but intertwined with science, geography, economics, and even art. This holistic approach ensures that students from a young age understand the complexities of environmental issues and the importance of sustainability. Lessons on climate change, resource conservation, and sustainable living are designed to empower students with the knowledge and skills they need to contribute to the environment positively.

Digital technology also plays a crucial role in greening the global classroom. The use of digital textbooks and resources can significantly reduce the need for paper, helping to conserve forests and reduce waste. Moreover, digital platforms enable schools to implement more dynamic and interactive forms of teaching that can adapt to include current environmental issues and debates, keeping the curriculum relevant and engaging. This not only helps in reducing the carbon footprint associated with traditional paper-based educational resources but also prepares students for a digital future.

The concept of a global classroom inherently supports sustainability through the promotion of cultural exchange and international cooperation on environmental issues. By connecting students from different parts of the world, schools can foster a sense of global community and shared responsibility towards the Earth.

Projects that involve international collaboration on sustainability initiatives can encourage students to think globally while acting locally, understanding that their actions contribute to a broader, collective environmental impact.

Sustainable practices also include the promotion of local and community-based learning. Schools are increasingly using their local environments as learning resources, encouraging students to engage with and improve their immediate surroundings. Outdoor education, community gardens, and local conservation projects help students make direct connections between their education and their environmental impact, fostering a sense of responsibility towards their local communities.

Furthermore, schools are embracing the concept of zero waste by implementing recycling programs, reducing single-use plastics, and managing food waste more effectively. These initiatives not only help reduce the environmental footprint of schools but also serve as practical, everyday lessons in sustainability for students.

Despite these positive steps, the path to fully green global classrooms is fraught with challenges. Economic constraints, especially in less developed areas, can impede the adoption of sustainable technologies and practices. There is also the challenge of ensuring that sustainability initiatives are inclusive and accessible to all students, regardless of their socio-economic background.

However, the movement towards sustainable practices in education is gaining momentum, driven by the growing recognition of environmental issues and the role education plays in addressing these challenges. As this trend continues, the global classroom will increasingly become a place where environmental education and sustainability are not just taught but are integral to the ethos and functioning of the institution.

In summary, greening the global classroom is about more than just teaching about the environment; it's about creating a culture of sustainability within educational institutions. This involves everything from the construction and operation of school buildings to the curriculum and daily activities. By embedding sustainable practices into all aspects of education, schools can not only reduce their environmental impact but also prepare students to be conscientious global citizens committed to living sustainably and protecting our planet.

ppp

"In the boundless classroom, diversity is celebrated, inclusion is embraced, and every voice is valued."

ƊƊƊ

EIGHT

Cultural Exchange: Lessons in Diversity and Inclusion

Cultural exchange in educational settings is essential for fostering lessons in diversity and inclusion. By integrating experiences that expose students to a variety of cultural perspectives, schools can create a more inclusive environment that celebrates differences and promotes mutual understanding. This approach is pivotal not only in educating students about global cultures but also in preparing them to thrive in a multicultural world.

Incorporating cultural exchange into the curriculum can take many forms, from language study and exchange programs to multicultural festivals and collaborative international projects. These experiences enable students to gain a deeper understanding of the world beyond their local community, challenging preconceptions and fostering a broader worldview.

Language education is often the first step in cultural exchange. By learning a new language, students do more than simply acquire communication skills; they also gain insights into the cultural contexts in which the language is spoken. This form of education encourages students to think critically about their own cultural norms and values, comparing them with those of other cultures. Language classes often include cultural components such as the study of literature, film, and art from target language countries, which help students appreciate the richness of other cultures.

International student exchange programs are perhaps the most immersive form of cultural exchange. Students who participate in these programs spend time living and studying in another country, which provides them with firsthand experience of a different culture. This immersion helps break down ethnic and cultural stereotypes and builds international relationships that can last a lifetime. For many, this experience is transformative, altering their perceptions of the world and their place within it.

Schools also facilitate cultural exchange through the celebration of international days and festivals, which serve to educate the student body about different cultures through food, music, dance, and storytelling. Such events not only provide fun and engaging ways to learn about different cultures but also help to foster a sense of community and belonging among students from diverse backgrounds. They allow students to express pride in their heritage and encourage others to appreciate and celebrate this diversity.

Collaborative projects involving students from different countries can also enhance cultural exchange. With the use of digital communication tools, students can work together on projects that address global issues such as climate change, poverty, and peacebuilding. These collaborations allow students to engage in dialogue with peers from around the world, offering multiple perspectives on critical issues and promoting a sense of global citizenship.

Moreover, the integration of multicultural education into the curriculum helps students understand the social, historical, and political contexts that shape different cultures. This type of education examines how identities are influenced by race, ethnicity, religion, and social status, among other factors. By understanding these dynamics, students become more empathetic and knowledgeable about the challenges faced by others. They are also better prepared to participate in discussions about social justice and equity, both locally and globally.

Teachers play a crucial role in fostering cultural exchange. They must be equipped to manage a diverse classroom, where students' varied backgrounds can lead to different—and sometimes conflicting—views and behaviors. Professional development in cultural competency is essential for teachers to effectively guide discussions on sensitive cultural issues and help build a classroom environment that respects and values diversity.

However, implementing effective cultural exchange programs presents challenges. These can include language barriers, the potential for cultural misunderstandings, and resistance from communities that may feel threatened by the perceived undermining of local cultural values. Furthermore, economic disparities can limit the ability of some students to participate in international exchange programs.

Despite these challenges, the benefits of cultural exchange in education are immense. It prepares students to succeed in a globalized world where cross-cultural communication and collaboration are often key to personal and professional success. Schools that embrace cultural exchange contribute to the development of open-minded, culturally aware graduates who are likely to become leaders in promoting inclusivity and diversity in their future endeavors.

In essence, cultural exchange in education is about more than just learning about other cultures; it's about using those insights to build a more inclusive and empathetic world. By emphasizing diversity and inclusion within the classroom, educators can play a vital role in shaping the global citizens of tomorrow, individuals who are not only aware of the world's diversity but who also value and celebrate it. This educational approach not only enriches students' lives but also helps to create a more just and connected world.

▷▷▷

"The future of education is collaborative, with teachers, students, families, and communities working together to create a more equitable and inclusive learning environment."

❦❦❦

NINE

Collaborative Learning: Strategies for Peer-to-Peer Education

Collaborative learning, a methodology that brings students together to solve problems, complete tasks, or gain understanding through collective effort, stands as a cornerstone of modern educational strategies. This approach not only enhances educational outcomes by pooling diverse thoughts and skills but also fosters essential interpersonal skills among learners. By engaging in peer-to-peer education, students learn to negotiate, communicate, and cooperate as part of a team, skills that are invaluable in both academic and real-world settings.

The essence of collaborative learning lies in its focus on group dynamics and interaction. Unlike traditional, lecture-based teaching methods where students are passive recipients of knowledge, collaborative learning involves them actively, requiring interaction, debate, and compromise. This active participation helps to deepen understanding as students explain concepts to each other, question their peers' reasoning, and jointly navigate towards solutions. This exchange often leads to greater retention of information and deeper understanding of the material because it engages multiple cognitive processes.

One effective strategy for implementing collaborative learning is through problem-based learning (PBL). In this approach, students are grouped and given a complex problem that doesn't have a straightforward solution. They must work together to research, apply various theories, and propose solutions based on their findings. This not only improves their ability to think critically and creatively but also mirrors real-world situations where problems are often ambiguous and require cooperation for resolution.

Another strategy is the use of collaborative projects, where students work together over extended periods on complex tasks, such as research projects, presentations, or community service initiatives. These projects require them to divide tasks, manage their time effectively, and often, integrate diverse skills and knowledge bases to produce a final product. Through such activities, students not only learn the subject matter more deeply but also develop project management and leadership skills.

Technology also plays a crucial role in facilitating collaborative learning, especially in today's globalized world. Digital tools and platforms such as forums, video conferencing, and shared document platforms allow students to collaborate across geographical boundaries. These technologies enable a form of asynchronous learning where students can contribute at different times, which is particularly beneficial for accommodating diverse schedules and learning paces. Moreover, such platforms often include features for tracking changes, providing feedback, and managing tasks, which can help in structuring and streamlining the collaborative process.

Peer teaching is another significant aspect of collaborative learning, where students take on the role of instructor for small segments of content. This method is based on the principle that teaching a concept is one of the best ways to learn it. In peer teaching scenarios, students prepare and deliver a lesson or a segment of a lesson, which helps them to understand the material thoroughly enough to explain it to others and answer questions. This not only reinforces the peer teacher's learning but also offers other students a different perspective on the material, often making it easier to understand.

Collaborative learning also encourages the development of soft skills such as empathy, listening, and giving and receiving constructive criticism. These social and emotional learning aspects are critical as they help students navigate interpersonal relationships and build a sense of community and belonging within the classroom. By learning to work with others, students prepare themselves for the collaborative nature of most modern work environments.

Despite its benefits, implementing collaborative learning can present challenges. It requires careful planning to ensure that groups are well-balanced and functional. There is also the risk of unequal participation, where dominant personalities might overshadow quieter ones. To mitigate this, educators must be adept at group management and use strategies such as assigning roles or using structured exercises to ensure that all students are actively participating and valued.

Collaborative learning represents a shift towards a more dynamic and democratic form of education. It acknowledges that learning can be a social endeavor and that students can contribute to each other's understanding and growth. By carefully implementing strategies that encourage effective collaboration, educators can create a learning environment that not only enhances academic achievement but also prepares students with the critical life skills needed for success beyond the classroom. As education continues to evolve, the importance of collaborative learning is likely to increase, reflecting the collaborative nature of global society and the professional world.

ᐺᐺᐺ

"By fostering a growth mindset in students, we empower them to embrace challenges, learn from failure, and persist in the pursuit of their goals."

❥❥❥

TEN
PROJECT-BASED LEARNING: SOLVING REAL-WORLD PROBLEMS

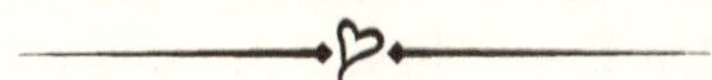

Project-based learning (PBL) is an instructional methodology that enables students to engage in extended learning experiences focused on real-world problems. This approach integrates knowing and doing, as students apply what they learn from academic disciplines to solve practical issues, gaining deep insights through active exploration and challenges. PBL not only promotes a deeper understanding of content but also develops essential skills such as critical thinking, collaboration, and communication.

At its core, project-based learning revolves around projects that are complex, require sustained attention, and involve questions or problems that mimic real-world challenges. These projects are typically student-centered, with learners given the autonomy to choose the methods and solutions they find most relevant and engaging. This autonomy enhances their motivation and investment in the learning process, making the educational experience more meaningful.

A well-designed PBL experience starts with a question or problem that is open-ended, relevant, and challenging. For example, students might be asked to design a cost-effective, sustainable home for a specific climate and demographic. This task would require them to research climate considerations, sustainable building materials, and demographic needs, integrating knowledge from subjects such as geography, economics, science, and engineering. As they develop their project, students must also consider their design's feasibility, cost, and impact on the community and environment, requiring a deep dive into practical and ethical considerations.

The process of project-based learning typically follows several key steps: beginning with an introduction to the problem, followed by planning, research, and execution, culminating in a final presentation. During these phases, students collaborate, critique each other's ideas, and iterate on their solutions. Teachers act as facilitators, providing guidance and resources, pushing students to think critically, and challenging them to go deeper into their investigations.

Collaboration is a critical component of PBL. By working in teams, students learn to communicate effectively, delegate tasks, manage conflicts, and support each other's learning. This collaborative environment mirrors the real world, where complex problems are rarely solved by individuals working in isolation. Instead, team-based approaches are common, requiring individuals to contribute their unique skills and perspectives towards a common goal.

Moreover, PBL allows for the integration of technology in meaningful ways. Students might use digital tools for research, collaboration, design, and presentation. For instance, they might use CAD software for design, spreadsheets for budgeting, or video editing software for presenting their projects. The use of technology not only supports the learning process but also helps students develop digital literacy skills critical in today's tech-driven world.

Assessment in PBL is another area where traditional practices are rethought. Instead of relying solely on tests and quizzes, assessment in PBL environments often includes peer and self-assessment, teacher observations, and the evaluation of project artifacts. These assessments focus on both the product and the process, including how well students collaborate, solve problems, and apply their knowledge. This comprehensive approach ensures that assessments are authentic and aligned with the skills and knowledge that students are expected to acquire.

Despite its many benefits, implementing project-based learning can be challenging. It requires teachers to shift from being sources of knowledge to facilitators of learning, which can be a significant transition for those accustomed to traditional teaching methods. There is also the challenge of ensuring that projects are sufficiently rigorous and aligned with academic standards. Additionally, PBL requires significant planning and resources, which can be a barrier in under-resourced educational settings.

However, the benefits of project-based learning make it a compelling choice for modern education. By engaging students in solving real-world problems, PBL prepares them for the complexities of the real world. They not only learn academic content more deeply but also acquire practical skills that are highly valued in the workplace. Furthermore, PBL can make learning more engaging and relevant, helping students see the connection between their education and the world they live in.

Project-based learning represents a significant shift in educational practices, focusing on preparing students not just to pass tests, but to solve problems, think critically, and collaborate effectively. As education continues to evolve, the principles of PBL offer a promising path toward more dynamic, relevant, and effective learning experiences.

❧❧❧

"Innovation is the engine that drives progress in education, opening up new possibilities for personalized learning, collaboration, and engagement."

ᕤᕤᕤ

ELEVEN

LANGUAGE LEARNING: TOOLS FOR GLOBAL COMMUNICATION

Language learning is increasingly viewed not just as an academic discipline, but as a crucial tool for global communication and cultural understanding. In our interconnected world, the ability to communicate in multiple languages is more than a practical necessity; it fosters greater international collaboration and understanding. With advances in technology and pedagogy, the methods and tools available for language learning have expanded dramatically, making it more accessible and effective than ever before.

The traditional model of language learning often involved rote memorization and repetitive grammar drills, which could be both tedious and inefficient. However, contemporary approaches emphasize immersive, interactive, and context-based learning, which are more engaging and effective. These methods reflect a broader shift in understanding how languages are best learned and the role technology can play in that process.

One of the most revolutionary tools for language learning has been the development of language learning apps and software. Platforms like Duolingo, Babbel, and Rosetta Stone use interactive exercises and adaptive technology to tailor lessons to the learner's pace and level of knowledge. These tools incorporate listening, speaking, reading, and writing exercises, providing a comprehensive language learning experience. They also utilize gamification to motivate learners by tracking progress, awarding points, and leveling up as one's skills improve. This approach not only makes learning more engaging but also allows learners to see tangible progress in their language abilities.

Another significant advancement in language learning tools is the use of virtual reality (VR). VR offers an immersive experience that simulates real-life interactions and scenarios in which language skills can be practiced. For example, VR can transport users to a virtual market in a Spanish-speaking country, where they must converse with vendors in Spanish to complete their shopping. This kind of contextual learning helps students apply their language skills in practical, everyday situations, significantly enhancing their ability to remember and use what they learn.

Online language exchange platforms are another innovative tool that facilitates real-time communication with native speakers around the world. Websites and apps like Tandem and HelloTalk connect learners with native speakers who are learning their language, allowing both parties to practice their new language skills in natural, conversational settings. This method not only improves language proficiency but also helps learners gain insights into the cultural nuances of the language, which are often as important as grammar and vocabulary.

Artificial intelligence (AI) is also transforming language learning by providing personalized learning experiences. AI-powered chatbots can converse with learners in the target language, offering corrections and suggestions in real-time. These bots can adapt their responses based on the learner's proficiency level, ensuring that the conversation remains challenging yet comprehensible. AI can also analyze speech patterns and provide feedback on pronunciation, helping learners improve their speaking skills more effectively.

Furthermore, online courses and virtual classrooms have made language learning more accessible to people around the world. Universities and independent language schools offer online language courses that can be accessed anywhere, providing flexibility for learners who may not be able to attend traditional classes. These courses often include live sessions with instructors, peer interactions, and access to extensive learning materials, combining the structure of classroom learning with the convenience of online access.

Despite these advancements, language learning remains a challenging endeavor that requires consistent practice and exposure. The most effective language learning experiences are those that are immersive, allowing learners to use the language in a variety of contexts and for different purposes. It is also important for learners to be exposed to different dialects and styles of communication within the language to build a comprehensive understanding.

In summary, the tools for language learning have evolved significantly, providing learners with a range of options that can be tailored to their needs and preferences. From apps and online courses to VR experiences and AI tutors, the resources available today support a more interactive, engaging, and effective approach to language learning. These advancements not only enhance the learning process but also contribute to greater cultural understanding and cooperation in our increasingly globalized world. By equipping individuals with the tools to communicate across languages, we are paving the way for more interconnected and empathetic global interactions.

ƿƿƿ

"Global competence is essential for success in the 21st century, empowering students to understand and navigate the complexities of an interconnected world."

❧❧❧

TWELVE

STEM AND BEYOND: ENCOURAGING INNOVATION IN CORE SUBJECTS

The emphasis on Science, Technology, Engineering, and Mathematics (STEM) education is pivotal in preparing students for the demands of the 21st-century workforce and encouraging innovation across these critical domains. STEM education integrates these core subjects into a cohesive learning model based on real-world applications, fostering not only a deeper understanding but also a greater enthusiasm for scientific and technological advancements. As economies become increasingly reliant on technology and scientific innovation, education systems worldwide recognize the need to bolster STEM programs and extend their reach to encompass new, interdisciplinary fields such as robotics, artificial intelligence, and biotechnology.

The foundation of effective STEM education is the integration of these disciplines in ways that encourage practical application. Traditional educational approaches often treat science and mathematics as isolated subjects, studied separately from their applications. However, by integrating these subjects into unified, project-based learning experiences, students can see the real-world relevance of their studies. For instance, a project might require students to design a simple machine. This would not only involve engineering principles but also the physics underlying the mechanics and the mathematical calculations needed to ensure the machine's functionality.

Innovation in STEM education also involves the use of cutting-edge technology in the classroom. This includes everything from computer simulations and virtual laboratories to 3D printing and robotics kits. These technologies allow students to experiment and learn in safe, cost-effective environments. Virtual labs, for example, can simulate chemical reactions, biological processes, and physical experiments that might be too dangerous or expensive to conduct in a school setting. Similarly, coding and robotics projects teach logical thinking and problem-solving skills that are essential for engineering and technology careers.

Beyond merely providing the tools and projects, encouraging innovation in STEM requires a pedagogical shift towards inquiry-based learning. This method centers on posing questions, problems, or scenarios rather than simply presenting established facts. Students are encouraged to research, experiment, and come to their own conclusions, which drives engagement and deep learning. For example, instead of teaching the laws of physics through textbook examples, students might be asked to design an experiment that demonstrates these laws in action.

The expansion of STEM to "STEAM" — which includes the Arts — is another innovation enhancing core subjects. This approach acknowledges the role of creativity and design thinking in scientific and technological innovation. The Arts encourage creative problem-solving and can make STEM subjects more accessible to students who might not otherwise be interested. By integrating artistic design into a technology project, for example, students can explore new and creative uses for technology that go beyond traditional applications.

Collaborative learning environments are also crucial in fostering innovation. When students work together on STEM projects, they share different perspectives and skills, enhancing the learning experience for everyone involved. This collaboration mirrors the real-world environment in high-tech industries, where team-based projects are the norm. Schools are increasingly using maker spaces, shared laboratories, and group projects to encourage a collaborative approach to STEM education.

Furthermore, the role of educators in STEM fields is evolving from instructors to facilitators of learning. Teachers are increasingly required to guide rather than dictate the learning process, providing resources and support while allowing students to take the lead in their own learning. Professional development for teachers is crucial in this regard, as they must be up-to-date with the latest scientific and technological advancements to effectively guide their students.

Challenges remain in implementing effective STEM education. These include disparities in resources between schools, which can affect the quality of STEM learning, and the ongoing need to update curricula to keep pace with rapidly changing technologies. Additionally, there is the challenge of ensuring that STEM education is inclusive and accessible to all students, regardless of gender, race, or socioeconomic background.

In summary, fostering innovation in STEM and beyond requires a multi-faceted approach: integrating technology, adopting inquiry-based learning models, expanding to include the Arts, and fostering collaborative environments. These strategies not only enhance the learning and teaching of core subjects but also prepare students to be creative, critical thinkers capable of tackling complex problems. As STEM fields continue to drive global innovation, education systems must adapt to prepare students not just to participate in but to lead the advancements of tomorrow.

ᐅᐅᐅ

"As educators, our job is not just to teach content,
but to instill in students a love of learning that will
last a lifetime."

❦❦❦

THIRTEEN

CREATIVE ARTS: EXPANDING MINDS BEYOND BORDERS

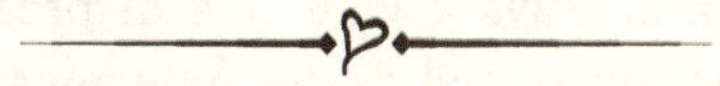

The creative arts play a crucial role in expanding minds beyond borders, offering a profound medium for expression, communication, and cultural exchange. As an integral component of education, the arts challenge students to think creatively and critically, fostering skills that are applicable across numerous disciplines and in daily life. By engaging in the arts, students develop a greater understanding of diverse cultures and histories, enhancing their empathy and global awareness.

Creative arts education encompasses a wide range of disciplines, including visual arts, music, dance, and theater. Each discipline offers unique benefits and learning opportunities. For instance, visual arts allow students to explore concepts of color, form, and perspective, which can be tools for communication that transcend linguistic barriers. Music, encompassing both performance and appreciation, can evoke emotional responses and foster connections among individuals from varying backgrounds. Dance and theater, as forms of physical expression and storytelling, provide platforms for understanding and expressing complex social and personal issues.

In the realm of visual arts, students learn to interpret and create visual messages. Art classes teach more than just the technical skills of drawing, painting, or sculpting; they encourage students to convey ideas and emotions through visual media. This form of expression is particularly powerful in a globalized world, where images are central to media and communication. Through projects that require the representation of different cultures, themes, or global issues, students gain insights into the ways in which images shape our understanding of the world.

Music education also plays a vital role in broadening students' horizons. Learning about and performing music from different cultures can be a direct entry point into those cultures' histories and traditions. Furthermore, music has a unique capacity to cross cultural divides, creating a shared experience that can promote unity and understanding. Collaborative music projects, such as international youth orchestras or school band exchanges, not only provide opportunities for cultural exchange but also teach the value of teamwork and respect for diverse viewpoints.

Dance and theater similarly offer significant opportunities for personal and social development. Through these disciplines, students explore the concept of narrative and the use of body language and space to tell stories. Participating in a theater production or a dance performance requires understanding characters and narratives that may be rooted in cultural contexts different from one's own. This not only enriches the student's artistic and cultural knowledge but also enhances their ability to empathize with others.

Beyond the intrinsic value of the arts, integrating creative disciplines into education encourages a holistic approach to learning. The creative arts emphasize critical thinking and problem-solving skills, as students must often conceptualize and execute projects from start to finish. This process fosters a type of innovative thinking that is beneficial in any academic or professional field. For example, the planning and execution involved in a school art exhibition can teach students valuable lessons in project management and logistical planning.

The benefits of arts education are also evident in the development of soft skills, such as communication and collaboration. Arts projects frequently require students to work together, share ideas, and provide feedback. This collaborative process is critical in the professional world, where effective teamwork and communication are keys to success. Furthermore, presenting artwork or performing on stage can significantly enhance public speaking and presentation skills.

Despite these benefits, arts education often faces challenges, including funding cuts and a lower prioritization compared to STEM subjects. However, the value of integrating the arts into educational systems cannot be underestimated. The arts provide a vital balance, fostering creative expression and critical thinking that complement the analytical skills emphasized in other subjects.

The creative arts are essential for a well-rounded education, preparing students to engage with the world in thoughtful, innovative, and culturally aware ways. By expanding minds beyond borders, the arts play a critical role in developing not only educated individuals but also empathetic and culturally sensitive citizens. As globalization continues to connect various parts of the world, the importance of arts education in fostering an understanding and appreciation of this diversity cannot be overstated. Through the creative arts, students gain the tools necessary to navigate and contribute to an increasingly complex global society.

པ པ པ

"*Every child is unique, with their own strengths, challenges, and potential waiting to be unlocked.*"

❥❥❥

FOURTEEN

HEALTH AND WELLNESS: INTEGRATING MINDFULNESS INTO THE CURRICULUM

Integrating health and wellness, particularly mindfulness, into the curriculum is becoming increasingly recognized as essential for fostering holistic student development. This integration helps students cultivate mental resilience, emotional intelligence, and a heightened awareness of both self and others, which are crucial for both academic success and overall well-being. By incorporating mindfulness into daily educational practices, schools can offer students valuable tools to manage stress, improve concentration, and enhance cognitive outcomes.

Mindfulness involves a conscious focus on the present moment while acknowledging and accepting one's feelings, thoughts, and bodily sensations. It's a practice rooted in meditation, but its application extends far beyond this, encompassing a broad array of activities that help increase awareness and calmness. In educational settings, mindfulness can be implemented through guided meditations, mindful breathing exercises, and the integration of mindful moments throughout the school day.

The benefits of incorporating mindfulness into the curriculum are manifold. Research indicates that mindfulness can significantly reduce stress and anxiety, which are increasingly prevalent among students of all ages due to various pressures related to performance, social dynamics, and, more recently, the global uncertainty stemming from events like the COVID-19 pandemic. Through mindfulness exercises, students learn to manage their stress responses and develop greater emotional regulation. For example, simple breathing techniques can help students calm their minds and gain composure before exams or presentations, directly impacting their ability to perform under pressure.

Furthermore, mindfulness practices have been shown to improve students' attention and concentration, which are critical for learning. Mindful meditation, for instance, trains the brain to focus on the present moment and minimizes distractions. This heightened focus can enhance cognitive processes such as memory retention and understanding, ultimately supporting academic achievement. Teachers can facilitate this by starting classes with a short mindfulness exercise, setting a focused and calm tone for the lesson that follows.

Integrating mindfulness into the curriculum also supports social and emotional learning (SEL), a critical component of modern education that emphasizes the development of skills such as empathy, cooperation, and conflict resolution. Mindfulness encourages students to become more aware of their thoughts and emotions and to understand how these can affect their interactions with others. This self-awareness is a key aspect of emotional intelligence, enabling students to better navigate social complexities, build more positive relationships, and create supportive environments.

Moreover, the practice of mindfulness can lead to long-term health benefits. By reducing stress and its associated physiological impacts, mindfulness can contribute to better immune function, lower blood pressure, and improved sleep. These benefits not only enhance students' current academic performance and well-being but also contribute to their long-term health and productivity.

However, the challenge lies in effectively integrating mindfulness into a curriculum that is often already crowded and under pressure to meet academic standards. To overcome this, schools can start by incorporating short mindfulness activities that do not require extensive time, such as one-minute breathing exercises between classes or brief sessions of guided imagery during assemblies. Teacher training is also crucial, as educators need to understand and personally engage with mindfulness to effectively teach and model it for their students.

Additionally, the integration of mindfulness should be mindful of cultural and individual differences. Mindfulness practices can vary widely, and what works for one student may not suit another. Educators must be sensitive to these differences and offer a variety of mindfulness tools so that all students can find practices that resonate with them.

In summary, the inclusion of mindfulness in the curriculum is not merely an educational trend but a response to the growing need for approaches that address the mental, emotional, and physical health of students. By teaching students how to be mindful, schools equip them with essential skills for managing stress, enhancing academic performance, and navigating the complexities of social interactions. This holistic approach not only fosters healthier, more resilient individuals but also creates more conducive learning environments that can adapt to the diverse needs of all students. As mindfulness becomes increasingly embedded in educational settings, it promises to significantly impact the well-being and success of future generations.

ppp

"The boundless classroom is a place where curiosity is encouraged, questions are welcomed, and learning is a lifelong journey."

ヅヅヅ

FIFTEEN

Assessment Innovations: Beyond Standardized Tests

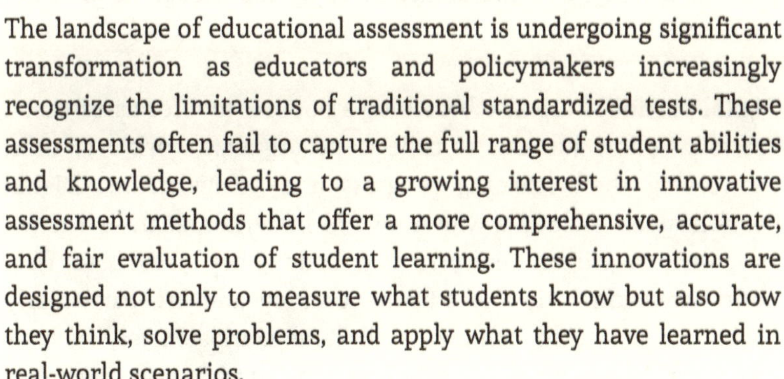

The landscape of educational assessment is undergoing significant transformation as educators and policymakers increasingly recognize the limitations of traditional standardized tests. These assessments often fail to capture the full range of student abilities and knowledge, leading to a growing interest in innovative assessment methods that offer a more comprehensive, accurate, and fair evaluation of student learning. These innovations are designed not only to measure what students know but also how they think, solve problems, and apply what they have learned in real-world scenarios.

One of the most prominent shifts in educational assessment is the move towards formative assessments as opposed to solely relying on summative, standardized tests. Formative assessments are integrated into the learning process, offering regular feedback that helps students understand their progress and areas needing improvement. This approach contrasts with summative assessments, which typically occur at the end of a learning period and provide a final evaluation of student learning. Formative assessments include quizzes, student reflections, discussions, and informal checks for understanding during lessons. These activities provide immediate insights into student comprehension and learning needs, allowing teachers to adjust instruction dynamically to better meet the needs of their students.

Another innovative approach gaining traction is performance-based assessment. This method requires students to demonstrate their knowledge and skills through complex tasks, often mirroring the types of problems they will face outside of school. For example, instead of simply testing a student's knowledge of scientific concepts through multiple-choice questions, a performance-based assessment might require the student to design and conduct an experiment to solve a real-world problem. This type of assessment evaluates not only factual knowledge but also critical thinking, problem-solving, and the ability to apply knowledge in practical contexts.

Digital portfolios are also becoming a popular tool for assessment. Portfolios allow students to collect and organize work over time, showcasing their learning progress and achievements. Digital portfolios can include a wide range of materials, such as written assignments, videos, artwork, and code. They provide a rich, multidimensional view of student learning and are particularly useful for assessing complex skills and competencies, such as creativity, leadership, and collaboration. Importantly, portfolios empower students by involving them directly in the assessment process, encouraging them to reflect on their own learning and growth.

Peer assessment is another assessment innovation that enhances learning by involving students in evaluating each other's work. This method helps students develop critical analysis skills and gain insight from their peers' perspectives. Peer assessment can be particularly effective in collaborative projects and presentations, where students can assess each other's contributions and provide constructive feedback. This process not only helps learners engage more deeply with the material but also fosters a sense of responsibility and accountability among students.

Self-assessment, closely related to peer assessment, is a method that encourages students to evaluate their own work against set criteria. This practice develops self-regulatory and reflective skills, helping students become more aware of their learning processes and progress. Self-assessment encourages a deeper connection to learning, as students identify their strengths and weaknesses and set personal goals for improvement.

Adaptive testing is a more technologically advanced innovation in assessment. These tests adjust the difficulty of questions based on the student's responses as the test progresses. Such assessments are typically computer-based and use algorithms to estimate a student's knowledge level, providing a more personalized assessment experience. Adaptive tests can more accurately measure a student's abilities, especially at the extremes of the ability spectrum, where traditional tests might not have enough challenging or supportive questions to gauge an individual's true capabilities.

While these innovations offer significant advantages over traditional standardized tests, their implementation is not without challenges. There is often a need for significant training for educators to effectively utilize these new methods. Additionally, these approaches require more time and resources than traditional tests, which can be a barrier for many schools. However, the benefits of a more accurate and holistic assessment of student learning make the investment worthwhile.

In summary, the field of educational assessment is evolving from a focus on standardized testing to a more diversified and nuanced approach. Innovations like formative assessments, performance-based tasks, digital portfolios, peer and self-assessment, and adaptive testing are reshaping how educators measure learning. These methods not only provide a richer and more accurate understanding of student abilities but also enhance the learning process itself by making assessment an integral part of education rather than a detached, anxiety-inducing event. As these innovative practices become more widespread, they promise to transform education into a more adaptive and inclusive system that recognizes and nurtures the diverse talents of all students.

"Technology is a powerful tool for learning, but it's the human connection between teacher and student that truly transforms lives."

❤❤❤

SIXTEEN

Teacher Training: Equipping Educators for a New Era

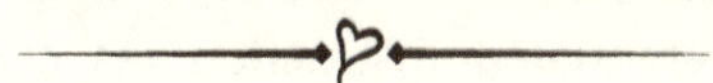

As the landscape of education continues to evolve, so too must the approach to teacher training. Today's educators are not just imparting knowledge; they are preparing students for a rapidly changing world, equipping them with critical thinking skills, and fostering creativity and innovation. This requires a new era of teacher training that emphasizes not only subject expertise but also pedagogical flexibility, technological proficiency, and an understanding of diverse learning needs and environments.

Effective teacher training programs are foundational to this vision. They must provide educators with the tools and strategies to handle a variety of classroom situations, including the integration of technology, the management of diverse classrooms, and the implementation of new educational paradigms such as project-based learning and flipped classrooms. Moreover, with the increasing recognition of the importance of social and emotional learning, teacher training needs to encompass strategies for developing these essential skills in students.

One of the critical areas where teacher training is evolving is in the integration of technology in education. With digital tools becoming ubiquitous in learning environments, educators must be proficient in using technology not just as a means of delivering content, but as a way to enhance student learning and engagement. This includes training in managing online learning platforms, utilizing educational software, and incorporating digital resources into lesson plans. Furthermore, teachers must be prepared to deal with the challenges that come with technology use in the classroom, including issues of digital equity and the responsible use of online information.

Another significant aspect of modern teacher training is the emphasis on differentiated instruction. As classrooms become increasingly diverse, educators must be able to adapt their teaching methods to meet the varied learning styles, abilities, and backgrounds of their students. This involves training in assessing student needs and customizing lessons to enhance learning outcomes for all students. Techniques such as tiered assignments, visual aids, and collaborative group activities are just a few examples of how teachers can modify their instructional methods to accommodate diverse learners.

Furthermore, contemporary teacher training programs must also prepare educators to foster critical thinking and problem-solving skills. This involves moving beyond rote memorization and encouraging students to analyze information, question assumptions, and develop their own conclusions. Training educators in inquiry-based learning, where students learn through exploring questions and problems, is vital. This approach not only engages students more deeply but also helps them develop the analytical skills necessary for success in today's information-rich world.

Social and emotional learning (SEL) is another crucial component of modern education that should be integrated into teacher training. Educators need to understand how to build and manage healthy, supportive classroom environments where students feel safe and valued. Training in SEL can equip teachers with the skills to enhance students' emotional intelligence, which is critical for personal and academic success. This includes strategies for managing classroom dynamics, teaching conflict resolution, and fostering an inclusive atmosphere that respects and celebrates diversity.

Additionally, teacher training programs must emphasize lifelong learning and professional development. The rapid pace of change in educational technology and pedagogy means that the learning process does not end with initial teacher certification. Ongoing professional development opportunities are essential for teachers to stay current with new teaching tools, educational research, and best practices. This can include workshops, conferences, online courses, and peer collaboration networks.

Implementing these advanced training strategies requires significant resources and commitment from educational institutions. It also demands a shift in how teacher effectiveness is assessed, moving away from traditional metrics like student test scores to more holistic evaluations that consider a teacher's ability to adapt to diverse classroom needs, integrate new learning technologies, and foster a supportive and inclusive learning environment.

In summary, the training of teachers for a new era of education is about equipping them with a diverse set of skills that go beyond traditional teaching methods. It involves preparing them to handle technological integration, diverse classrooms, and the fostering of critical thinking and social-emotional skills among their students. By focusing on these areas, teacher training programs can ensure that educators are not only capable of teaching the curriculum but also of playing a pivotal role in the holistic development of their students. As the demands on education continue to evolve, so too must the preparation of those at the forefront of teaching, ensuring they are ready to meet the challenges of this dynamic and crucial profession.

ppp

"Education is not just about preparing students for the future—it's about empowering them to shape it."

❦❦❦

SEVENTEEN

EDUCATIONAL EQUITY: BRIDGING THE GAP IN GLOBAL EDUCATION

Educational equity, the concept of ensuring that every student has access to the resources, opportunities, and support needed to succeed, is a fundamental pillar of a just and equitable society. Yet, despite significant progress in expanding access to education worldwide, disparities persist, both within and across countries. Addressing these disparities and bridging the gap in global education is essential not only for promoting social justice but also for fostering economic development, political stability, and overall societal well-being.

One of the most significant barriers to educational equity is economic inequality. In many parts of the world, access to quality education is directly linked to socioeconomic status. Children from low-income families often lack access to basic resources such as textbooks, technology, and transportation, which can significantly hinder their ability to succeed in school. Furthermore, they may face additional challenges outside the classroom, such as inadequate nutrition, unstable housing, or family responsibilities, which can further impact their educational outcomes.

To address economic disparities in education, governments and policymakers must prioritize investments in education infrastructure and resources, particularly in underserved communities. This includes ensuring equitable funding for schools, providing free or subsidized meals for students from low-income families, and expanding access to technology and internet connectivity. Additionally, targeted interventions such as early childhood education programs and support services for at-risk students can help level the playing field and ensure that all students have the opportunity to thrive academically.

Educational equity also encompasses issues of access and representation for marginalized and underserved populations, including racial and ethnic minorities, indigenous communities, girls and women, and individuals with disabilities. These groups often face systemic barriers that limit their access to quality education and perpetuate cycles of poverty and inequality. Addressing these barriers requires intentional efforts to dismantle discriminatory policies and practices, promote diversity and inclusion in educational settings, and ensure that all students have access to culturally relevant and affirming curriculum and resources.

Furthermore, educational equity requires a commitment to addressing disparities in educational outcomes. While access to education is essential, it is equally important to ensure that all students have the opportunity to succeed academically and achieve their full potential. This requires addressing disparities in academic achievement, graduation rates, and post-secondary outcomes among different demographic groups. It also involves providing targeted support and interventions for students who are struggling academically, such as tutoring, mentoring, and academic enrichment programs.

Another critical aspect of educational equity is addressing the digital divide, the gap between those who have access to technology and the internet and those who do not. In today's increasingly digital world, access to technology and digital literacy skills are essential for academic success and future economic opportunities. Yet, millions of students around the world lack access to reliable internet connectivity or devices such as computers or tablets. This disparity has been exacerbated by the COVID-19 pandemic, which forced many schools to transition to online learning, leaving behind those without access to technology.

To bridge the digital divide, governments and organizations must invest in expanding broadband infrastructure and providing devices and internet connectivity to underserved communities. Additionally, schools must prioritize digital literacy training for students and teachers to ensure that all members of the educational community can effectively navigate and utilize digital tools for learning. Efforts should also be made to develop and promote open educational resources that are accessible to all students, regardless of their socioeconomic background or geographic location.

Finally, achieving educational equity requires a commitment to addressing the root causes of inequality, including poverty, discrimination, and systemic oppression. This involves advocating for policies and practices that promote economic and social justice, such as living wage laws, affordable housing initiatives, and anti-discrimination legislation. It also requires challenging biases and stereotypes within educational institutions and promoting diversity, equity, and inclusion in all aspects of education.

Educational equity is essential for building a more just and equitable society. By addressing disparities in access, representation, outcomes, and resources, we can ensure that all students have the opportunity to succeed academically and achieve their full potential. Achieving educational equity requires a multi-faceted approach that involves targeted investments, policy reforms, and efforts to challenge systemic injustices. By working together to bridge the gap in global education, we can create a brighter and more equitable future for all students, regardless of their background or circumstances.

ppp

"The most effective educators are those who lead by example, inspiring students to dream big and reach for the stars."

ᗰᗰᗰ

EIGHTEEN

Parental and Community Involvement: Strengthening the Educational Ecosystem

Parental and community involvement in education play a crucial role in shaping the success and well-being of students. When parents, families, and communities are actively engaged in the educational process, students tend to perform better academically, exhibit improved behavior and attitudes towards learning, and experience greater overall success in school. Moreover, strong partnerships between schools and communities can help address systemic challenges, promote equity and inclusion, and create a more supportive and enriching educational ecosystem for all students.

At its core, parental involvement refers to the participation of parents and guardians in their children's education. This involvement can take many forms, including attending parent-teacher conferences, volunteering in classrooms, participating in school events, and supporting learning at home. Research consistently shows that students whose parents are actively involved in their education tend to have higher academic achievement, better attendance, and more positive attitudes towards school.

One of the key benefits of parental involvement is that it helps create a strong support system for students both at home and at school. When parents are engaged in their children's education, they demonstrate the value they place on learning and send a clear message that education is a priority. This positive reinforcement can have a significant impact on students' motivation and attitudes towards school, leading to increased academic success and a greater sense of belonging within the school community.

Moreover, parental involvement can help bridge the gap between home and school, creating a seamless learning environment that extends beyond the classroom. When parents are actively involved in their children's education, they are better equipped to support their learning at home, whether it's helping with homework, providing additional resources, or fostering a love of reading and learning. This partnership between home and school reinforces learning and helps students make meaningful connections between their academic experiences and their daily lives.

In addition to parental involvement, community engagement is also critical for strengthening the educational ecosystem. Communities play a vital role in supporting schools and students by providing resources, opportunities, and expertise that complement and enhance the educational experience. This can include partnerships with local businesses, nonprofit organizations, universities, and community groups to offer enrichment programs, internships, mentorships, and other learning opportunities outside of the classroom.

Community involvement in education also helps broaden students' perspectives and expose them to diverse experiences and career pathways. By connecting students with community members who have different backgrounds, skills, and expertise, schools can help students explore their interests, develop new talents, and envision possibilities for their future. Moreover, community partnerships can help address systemic challenges facing schools and students, such as poverty, inequality, and lack of access to resources, by leveraging community resources and expertise to provide additional support and services.

Furthermore, parental and community involvement in education can help promote equity and inclusion by ensuring that all students have access to the support, resources, and opportunities they need to succeed. This is particularly important for students from marginalized and underserved communities who may face additional barriers to academic success. By actively engaging parents, families, and communities in the educational process, schools can help create a more equitable and inclusive learning environment where all students have the opportunity to thrive.

However, fostering parental and community involvement in education is not without its challenges. Barriers such as language barriers, cultural differences, and lack of awareness or understanding about the importance of parental and community involvement can hinder efforts to engage families and communities in the educational process. Moreover, systemic inequities and disparities in access to resources and opportunities can further exacerbate these challenges, making it difficult for some families and communities to fully participate in their children's education.

To address these challenges and promote greater parental and community involvement in education, schools and communities must work together to build strong, collaborative partnerships based on trust, mutual respect, and shared goals. This requires proactive efforts to reach out to families and communities, listen to their needs and concerns, and involve them in decision-making processes that affect their children's education. It also involves providing resources, training, and support to help parents and community members become more actively engaged in the educational process.

Parental and community involvement in education are essential for creating a supportive, inclusive, and enriching educational ecosystem that promotes the success and well-being of all students. By actively engaging parents, families, and communities in the educational process, schools can help bridge the gap between home and school, promote equity and inclusion, and create a more holistic learning environment that prepares students for success in school and beyond. As schools and communities continue to work together to strengthen partnerships and build collaborative relationships, they can help ensure that every student has the support and resources they need to reach their full potential.

"In the boundless classroom, failure is not the end of the road, but the beginning of a new opportunity for growth and learning."

ꗏꗏꗏ

NINETEEN

FUTURE-PROOFING STUDENTS: SKILLS FOR A CHANGING WORLD

As we navigate the complexities of the 21st century, it's become increasingly clear that traditional educational paradigms are insufficient for preparing students for the challenges and opportunities of the future. The rapid pace of technological innovation, globalization, and societal change requires a new approach to education that prioritizes the development of skills and competencies that are essential for success in a rapidly changing world. Future-proofing students involves equipping them with the skills, knowledge, and mindset needed to thrive in an uncertain and dynamic environment, preparing them to adapt, innovate, and contribute meaningfully to society.

One of the key skills for future-proofing students is critical thinking. In a world inundated with information and misinformation, the ability to analyze, evaluate, and synthesize information critically is more important than ever. Critical thinking involves asking probing questions, examining evidence, considering multiple perspectives, and drawing well-reasoned conclusions. This skill is essential for making informed decisions, solving complex problems, and navigating the complexities of an increasingly interconnected and fast-paced world.

Similarly, creativity is another essential skill for future-proofing students. In a rapidly changing world, the ability to think creatively and innovatively is crucial for driving progress and solving complex challenges. Creativity involves thinking outside the box, generating novel ideas, and approaching problems from new angles. It also requires the willingness to take risks, experiment, and learn from failure. By fostering creativity in students, educators can empower them to adapt to change, embrace uncertainty, and seize opportunities for innovation and growth.

Collaboration and teamwork are also essential skills for future-proofing students. In today's interconnected world, the ability to work effectively with others from diverse backgrounds and perspectives is critical for success. Collaboration involves communication, cooperation, and compromise, as well as the ability to leverage the strengths of each team member to achieve common goals. By teaching students how to collaborate effectively, educators can prepare them to navigate complex social dynamics, build strong relationships, and work together towards shared objectives.

Another important skill for future-proofing students is adaptability. In a world characterized by rapid change and uncertainty, the ability to adapt to new situations, technologies, and environments is essential for success. Adaptability involves being flexible, resilient, and open-minded, as well as the willingness to learn and grow in response to new challenges and opportunities. By cultivating adaptability in students, educators can prepare them to navigate change with confidence and resilience, and to thrive in an ever-evolving world.

Furthermore, digital literacy is increasingly important for future-proofing students. In an era dominated by technology, the ability to use, understand, and evaluate digital tools and information is essential for success in school, work, and life. Digital literacy involves skills such as information literacy, media literacy, and technology literacy, as well as the ability to navigate online environments safely and responsibly. By teaching students how to be digitally literate, educators can empower them to harness the power of technology for learning, communication, and problem-solving.

In addition to these skills, future-proofing students also involves fostering a growth mindset. A growth mindset is the belief that intelligence, abilities, and talents can be developed through effort, practice, and perseverance. This mindset encourages students to embrace challenges, learn from failure, and persist in the face of obstacles. By cultivating a growth mindset in students, educators can help them develop resilience, self-confidence, and a love of learning that will serve them well throughout their lives.

Moreover, global competence is increasingly important for future-proofing students. In an interconnected world, the ability to understand and navigate global issues, cultures, and perspectives is essential for success. Global competence involves skills such as cultural awareness, empathy, and intercultural communication, as well as the ability to collaborate across borders and work effectively in diverse teams. By teaching students how to be globally competent, educators can prepare them to thrive in a multicultural world and contribute positively to global society.

Finally, future-proofing students involves fostering a sense of agency and purpose. In a world full of challenges and opportunities, it's important for students to develop a sense of agency—the belief that they have the power to make a difference in their own lives and in the world around them. This involves helping students identify their passions, interests, and values, and empowering them to pursue their goals with purpose and determination. By fostering agency and purpose in students, educators can inspire them to become lifelong learners, leaders, and changemakers who are committed to making a positive impact on the world.

Future-proofing students involves equipping them with a diverse set of skills, knowledge, and mindsets that are essential for success in a rapidly changing world. By prioritizing skills such as critical thinking, creativity, collaboration, adaptability, digital literacy, global competence, and a growth mindset, educators can prepare students to thrive in an uncertain and dynamic environment, and to contribute meaningfully to society. As we continue to navigate the challenges and opportunities of the 21st century, it's essential that we prioritize future-proofing students and empowering them to succeed in a rapidly evolving world.

"By embracing diversity and fostering inclusion, we
create a richer, more vibrant learning environment
where every student can thrive."

♥♥♥

TWENTY

The Role of Policy: Shaping the Future of Global Education

The role of policy in shaping the future of global education cannot be overstated. Educational policies at local, national, and international levels have a profound impact on the quality, accessibility, and equity of education systems around the world. They influence everything from curriculum standards and assessment practices to funding allocations and teacher training initiatives. As such, policy decisions have far-reaching implications for the future of education and the opportunities available to students.

At the heart of educational policy is the goal of ensuring that all students have access to a high-quality education that prepares them for success in school, work, and life. This requires policies that prioritize equity and inclusion, address systemic barriers to learning, and provide support and resources to those who need it most. Educational policies must also be responsive to the changing needs of students and communities, adapting to emerging trends and challenges in order to remain relevant and effective.

One of the key challenges facing educational policymakers is the need to address inequities in access to education. Despite significant progress in expanding access to education in recent decades, millions of children around the world still lack access to quality schooling due to factors such as poverty, discrimination, and conflict. To address these inequities, policymakers must prioritize investments in education infrastructure, provide targeted support for marginalized and underserved populations, and implement policies that promote diversity and inclusion in schools.

Furthermore, educational policies play a critical role in shaping curriculum standards and teaching practices. Curriculum policies determine what students are expected to learn and how that learning is assessed, while teaching policies dictate the qualifications, training, and support available to educators. By setting clear expectations for student learning and providing teachers with the tools and resources they need to be effective, educational policies can help ensure that all students receive a high-quality education that prepares them for success in the 21st century.

In addition to setting standards and expectations, educational policies also play a crucial role in determining how education is funded and resourced. Funding policies dictate how resources are allocated to schools and districts, including staffing levels, class sizes, and access to instructional materials and technology. By ensuring adequate and equitable funding for all schools, policymakers can help level the playing field and provide all students with the support they need to succeed.

Moreover, educational policies can also influence the ways in which schools and educators are held accountable for student learning outcomes. Accountability policies set expectations for student achievement and establish mechanisms for monitoring and evaluating school and teacher performance. While accountability is important for ensuring that schools are meeting the needs of students and taxpayers, policymakers must be mindful of the unintended consequences of high-stakes testing and other accountability measures, which can lead to teaching to the test, narrowing of the curriculum, and inequities in resource allocation.

Additionally, educational policies play a crucial role in shaping the future of global education by fostering collaboration and cooperation among countries. International education policies and initiatives, such as the Sustainable Development Goals for Education and the Education 2030 Agenda, provide a framework for global cooperation and action to improve access to quality education for all. By working together to share best practices, resources, and expertise, countries can help address common challenges and ensure that all children have the opportunity to learn and thrive.

However, crafting effective educational policies is not without its challenges. Policymakers must navigate competing interests and priorities, negotiate complex political dynamics, and consider the diverse needs and perspectives of stakeholders. Moreover, the pace of change in education, driven by factors such as technological innovation and globalization, requires policymakers to be agile and responsive to emerging trends and challenges.

The role of policy in shaping the future of global education is paramount. Educational policies influence everything from access to schooling and curriculum standards to teaching practices and resource allocation. By prioritizing equity and inclusion, setting clear expectations for student learning, ensuring adequate funding and support for schools and educators, and fostering collaboration and cooperation among countries, policymakers can help ensure that all children have access to a high-quality education that prepares them for success in the 21st century. As we continue to navigate the challenges and opportunities of the future, it is essential that policymakers remain committed to crafting policies that prioritize the needs of students and promote equity, excellence, and opportunity in education.

ϼϼϼ

"The future of education is bright, filled with endless possibilities for innovation, collaboration, and positive change."

❥❥❥

TWENTY-ONE
SUMMARY

The Boundless Classroom: Innovations in Global Education has explored a wide range of topics and innovations that are shaping the future of education worldwide. From the digital revolution to parental involvement, from personalized learning to policy shaping, each chapter has delved into key aspects of education in the 21st century. This summary chapter aims to distill the insights and lessons learned from the previous discussions and highlight the overarching themes and principles that are essential for creating a more equitable, inclusive, and effective educational system for all.

At the heart of the discussion is the recognition that education is undergoing a profound transformation driven by technological innovation, globalization, and societal change. The digital revolution, characterized by the widespread adoption of digital tools and technologies, has fundamentally changed the way we teach and learn. From virtual reality to artificial intelligence, technology has opened up new possibilities for personalized learning, collaboration, and engagement. However, while technology offers immense potential to enhance education, it also presents challenges such as the digital divide and the need for digital literacy skills.

Central to the discussion is the concept of educational equity—the idea that all students, regardless of their background or circumstances, should have access to a high-quality education. Achieving educational equity requires addressing systemic barriers such as poverty, discrimination, and lack of resources that prevent some students from reaching their full potential. It also involves promoting diversity and inclusion in schools and communities, ensuring that all students feel valued, respected, and supported.

Parental and community involvement are recognized as essential components of educational equity. When parents, families, and communities are actively engaged in the educational process, students tend to perform better academically, exhibit improved behavior and attitudes towards learning, and experience greater overall success in school. Moreover, strong partnerships between schools and communities can help address systemic challenges, promote equity and inclusion, and create a more supportive and enriching educational ecosystem for all students.

The discussion also highlights the importance of teacher training and professional development in shaping the future of education. Today's educators are not just imparting knowledge; they are preparing students for a rapidly changing world, equipping them with critical thinking skills, fostering creativity and innovation, and promoting diversity and inclusion. Effective teacher training programs are foundational to this vision, providing educators with the tools and strategies to handle diverse classrooms, integrate technology, and implement new educational paradigms.

Another key theme is the importance of fostering 21st-century skills such as critical thinking, creativity, collaboration, adaptability, and digital literacy. In a rapidly changing world, these skills are essential for success in school, work, and life. By prioritizing the development of these skills, educators can prepare students to thrive in an uncertain and dynamic environment, and to contribute meaningfully to society.

Finally, the role of policy in shaping the future of education cannot be overstated. Educational policies at local, national, and international levels have a profound impact on the quality, accessibility, and equity of education systems worldwide. By prioritizing equity and inclusion, setting clear expectations for student learning, ensuring adequate funding and support for schools and educators, and fostering collaboration and cooperation among countries, policymakers can help ensure that all children have access to a high-quality education that prepares them for success in the 21st century.

From technological innovation to parental involvement, from teacher training to policy shaping, each chapter has highlighted key principles and themes that are essential for creating a more equitable, inclusive, and effective educational system for all. By prioritizing equity, fostering 21st-century skills, and working together to address the challenges and opportunities of the future, we can ensure that every student has the opportunity to thrive and succeed in school and beyond.

ððð

Citation And References

This book represents the culmination of extensive research and meticulous analysis, incorporating a diverse range of sources, including numerous books, scholarly studies, and personal experiences. Additionally, I have scoured various websites to gather relevant information and data essential for the compilation of this work. I have taken every precaution to ensure the accuracy of the information presented and have diligently cited all sources to acknowledge their contributions.

Despite these efforts, the possibility of inadvertent errors remains. I deeply value the insights of my readers and appreciate any feedback that can help identify and rectify such inaccuracies. I encourage you to bring any discrepancies to my attention.

Your feedback is not only welcome but crucial, as it will aid in correcting current editions and enhancing the content of future ones. I am committed to maintaining the highest standards of accuracy and reliability in my work and thank you for your support and understanding.

Additionally, I firmly uphold the principle of freedom of speech and expression as guaranteed under Article 19(1)(a) of the Constitution of India, and I respect the diverse viewpoints and expressions of all readers.

誌誌誌

Other Books Of The Author

1. Empowering Minds: A Journey into Women's Self-Discovery and Power
2. The Dynamics of Motivation: Catalyzing Thought into Action
3. Meditation and Mental Well Being: The Path to Inner Peace and Clarity
4. The Psychology of Child Education: Nurturing Future Generations
5. Ethical Enlightenment: A Modern Guide to Living with Integrity
6. Voices of Empowerment: Stories of Women Rising Against Odds
7. Social Psychology in Everyday Life: Understanding Human Connections
8. The Essence of Motivational Speaking: Inspiring Change in Others
9. Balancing Acts: Women, Work, and the Will to Lead
10. Guiding with Grace: Raising Children with Compassion and Awareness
11. The Power of Positive Aging: Embracing Life After Fifty
12. Building Resilient Communities: Social Work in Action
13. The Ethical Educator: Principles for Teaching and Learning
14. From Insight to Impact: Social Psychology for a Better World
15. The Ethics of Empathy: A Guide to Ethical Living
16. The Science of Empowering the Self: Navigating Life's Challenges with Psychological Wisdom
17. The Mindful Conscious Leader: Meditation Techniques for Modern Management
18. Pioneering Spirit: Women's Pathways to Leadership and Empowerment
19. Feeling to Healing: The Role of Emotional Intelligence in Child Development
20. Transformative Talks and Words of Inspiration: Insights into Motivational Oratory

21. The Hidden Path to Ethical Sustainability: Crafting a Greener Tomorrow
22. Spiritual Integrity: Navigating Life with Moral Compassion
23. Clean Living, Clean Society: The Ethics of Cleanliness
24. Patriotic Spirits: Building a Nation on Positive Attitudes
25. Innovative Integrity & Vibrant Visions: The Ethical and Entrepreneurial Spirit of Gujarat
26. Youthful Visions, Endless Possibilities: Inspiring Ethics and Motivation in Children
27. Living Your Legacy: How to Motivate Others by Living Your Values
28. Secret of Healing Conversations: Ethical Practices in Counselling and Therapy
29. Creative Kindness: Crafting a Life of Compassion and Creativity
30. The Power of Appreciation: How Gratitude Can Transform Your Relationships
31. Bhagavad-Gita: Messages
32. Science of Art: The New Frontier of Fashion Modernism
33. Vivekananda's Virtues: A Blueprint for Modern Living
34. Empower Her: Navigating the Path to Women's Entrepreneurship
35. The Boundless Classroom: Innovations in Global Education
36. The Language of Leadership: Communicating with Authenticity and Impact
37. The Warrior's Mantra: Deciphering the Hanuman Chalisa
38. Echoes of Empathy: Transformative Stories of Social Service
39. Artful Living: Cultivating Creativity in Your Daily Routine
40. Finding Your Why: Discovering Your Passions and Charting Your Course
41. The Role of Social Media in Shaping Self-Esteem and Interpersonal Relationships among Adolescents

ЬЬЬ

Contact

Dr. Minakshi Bansal
Social Activist
Ahmedabad, Gujarat, Bharat
minakshiindiag20@yahoo.com

❧❧❧

|| LOKAHA SAMASTHAHA SUKHINO BHAVANTU ||